Screamings from

a maddening mind

Alan David Penrose

PublishAmerica
Baltimore

First printing

ISBN: 1-4241-1454-3
PUBLISHED BY PUBLISHAMERICA, LLLP
www.publishamerica.com
Baltimore

Printed in the United States of America

Contents

Foreword

Well, what can I say? That this is a dream come true? Well maybe, but the hell I have put myself through to get to this point is far too scary to recollect. Firstly I should apologise to all those I may have hurt along the way, but I too have been hurt. Now it's no excuse for what I have done, but it goes some way to explain it. It's human nature to treat people in the way we have been treated. And then again if I had not caused any harm or been harmed, would I have had anything to write about?

It has been said that you can't sing the blues until you have lived them, and wow, have I lived them. A lot was probably self-inflicted—I do have a self-destructive nature—but also a lot was inflicted on me. I don't blame anyone. It's just life—the repetition of boy meets girl, boy loses girl, boy finds new girl and loses girl; it's a never ending cycle of life. It's happening somewhere in this world as you read this. It doesn't get any easier as you get older, but alcohol plays a bigger part once you reach an age where you're able to get served.

Life has a strange way of changing when you least expect it.

Mine changed in a big way on the 17th March 2002. Joanne, my soul mate, love of my life and mother to my babies, left my world. That very night I went to the pub and there I stayed for two years. The poems that follow in some part chart my decline, in some part try to explain and in some part are my redemption from a twilight world of drugs, alcohol and depression. Cheery read, isn't it? But read these poems for what they are: my life laid bare.

Now please don't be scared; just enjoy the read for what it is: my emotional roller coaster. Life is not like a Hollywood movie, and if it were, would we all get bored? The eternal sunshine of the celluloid world flickers before our eyes at the movies; we're lost for a couple of hours in a world of popcorn, fizzy pop and special effects that stun and amaze. We leave believing we are Luke Skywalker, Indiana Jones or Vito Corleone. The real world only penetrates this bubble in the cold night air as we step back into real life and we are Mr Joe Average once more. We dream to live this life of fast cars and unlimited money, but when we get home to our two up, two down terrace house with washing up still in the sink from last night's dinner, the real world smacks you between the eyes.

In my humble opinion, in this life you just have to be grateful for what you have. I wake every morning and my boxer Henry gives me a kiss and wags his tail, and the look of love in his eyes warms my soul. Once it was my children—they think you're the best thing since sliced bread, and no matter what you do it never changes. My children, as bad as it now seems, have seen me in states that I should never have been seen in, and they in their childlike innocence accept and move on. We should, as adults, take a leaf from their book.

Life is a series of challenges that we must all overcome to the best of our mortal ability. So, you're short, you're fat, you're too tall, you will never play for a national team or you're not blessed with any redeeming features—we all have our place and part to play in this life. I'm no different from you, or the guy down the street who brushes the pavement. I don't pretend to be. We will never know what part we are to play in this life. The film *It's a Wonderful Life* will always explain it better than I.

But I love my life. I have learnt who and what I am. I may never be famous, I may never be rich, but I am loved, and that means more to me than any gold in the world. I have the memories of being loved intensely by my ex-wife and being loved completely by my babies. Even the most humble of men has riches in this life beyond the monetary kind. When I finally reach my end of days, I will close my eyes and see my happy times projected on the inside of my eyelids, a personal picture show in golden tints of autumn, and as I lay there and smile, waiting for my last gasp, I will be in my heaven. Let those around me look on in wonder and only remember the happier times. Because at the end of the day, that's what we will all take with us to the next life— no money or treasured possessions, no picture to say I was there. And when our children and grandchildren go, we will be forgotten to this world; just dust and browning pieces of paper will be all that's left to show we were ever here, washed out like a gravy stain on the shirt of life. It will keep going with or without us, so enjoy the sunsets you see and the stars that sparkle in their own universes, and take that memory with you to the end of your days. It's worth more to you than the money in your pocket.

This book is dedicated to all the people who help me through the hard times. You all know who you are and how you helped. It is with many thanks to you that I arrived at this place and at this time. Also to Alicia, Alexander and Octavia, my children; you are my love, my life and my babies. Thank you for never giving up on me, even at my lowest times. I have always and will always love you.

And lastly a special thanks goes to John Pitt, a magician with the optical art. Anyone who can make me look acceptable with a camera is a star indeed.

Alan David Penrose
_____

Leaving my life behind

I drive the long black highway,
cutting a swath through this green isle,
like cancerous decaying veins,
its tin and glass worlds gliding along,
the music in mine droning out as my mind wanders,
passing by fields of green and cathedral cities,
minutes passing by into the atmosphere of history,
as many before them,
moments before in this world of mine,
filled with the laughter of small children,
my heart was bursting with the joy of a small child on
Christmas Eve,
but now as the miles disappear behind me,
the distance growing ever greater,
my world changes back to the emptiness as before,
closer to the prison of my singleness.

the sun sets to the warming tones of summer,
although my core grows the coldness of mid winter,
the trees I pass in their early spring glory,
set stark almost out of place,

against the backdrop of black tarmac and grey concrete their
boundary,
the green fields and yellow rape I pass try to cheer me,
as the frost sets into my heart once again.

my mind drifts back again to a time,
when moments of happiness were less fleeting and short-lived,
the warming glow of my children's smiles lit my world,
like hot August sun burning my skin,
when my tears were warm from joy,
not poisoned from sadness and regret.

my mind cruelly snapped back by the harshness of scathing
blue signs,
pointing my way back to loneliness,
screaming at me in their own bludgeoning way,
clawing at my soul,
as the reapers will in time,
calling me to nothingness and solitude of my death,
but in this calling,
the emptiness of a living death
as only the smiles of my children make me come alive,
like a warming sweet kiss of life to my spirit,
until next time I am leaving my life behind

May 4th 2004

My demons

We all have our demons,
This is mine,

My demons I once quenched with a silky sweet nectar,
Now linger inside,
Trapped and screaming,
Louder day by day,
I fear to let them out,
In case they engulf me totally,
But my will weakens,
Giving in to them come nightfall,
Now no longer able to control,
Giving in to the need to silence them,
In my torment they revel,
Drink to forget,
But just for the shortest of time,
Helping me to put the past behind,
If only for one night,
The black cloud now rising to smother my will to resist,
Just one for the smallest relief from my pain,
My aching heart soon to be filled with a drunken joy,

Only a masquerade mask to cover my pain,
In a purple haze of fun,
Once again the painted smile of the clown,
My will easily bent,
My grief just covered with the silky satin veil soon to pass,
Now just left with the maddening shriek of a million dark crows,
Pecking at my tender mind,
Giving way and returning to my demons,
Through the day,
To torture my soul,
Only to begin again and set them free come dark.

May 5th 2004

Emptiness

A house that once resonated with the joy of children,
Now stands still and silent.
These walls close in more day by day,
Claustrophobia playing tricks with my mind,
A swirling black cloud of despair,
Choking my will to live,
Draining my will to carry on.

I search for rhyme and reason,
In this life now bestowed on me,
A reason to rise from my slumber,
Looking forward to a time with relish,
When life calls me back,
And this horror will be over.

I find no solace in the despair of those who done me wrong,
She thought the grass was greener,
Just to find a barren field,
A life thrown away for an image of perfection,
A mirage in the desert of his reality.

So here I sit in my colourless world,
Sepia tones haunt my waking hours,
No spring chicken, I'm afraid
Will I end my days crushed by these encroaching walls,
Will some beauty bring my colour back and save me.

Spring time unfolds outside my window,
But doesn't make it past the sill,
Trees with young new leaves beckon me back to life,
My heart destroyed and soul crippled,
Will I ever trust again,
Does love exist,
I'm broken and alone,
Unable to fix,
Living in this world of emptiness.

May 6th 2004

Henry

In this life of hollow repetition,
There is only one thing that keeps me going,
It is love in the purest of forms, not contaminated by hate or
loathing,

Though I may not do right,
Though I may not be perfect,
It is an undying love,
On which I may rely.

Come hell or high water,
Come infidelity or misbehaviour,
Drunkenness or debauchery,
There is one love that will remain strong.

If I die soon,
Will his heart break,
Will he pine away to be with me once more,
Will his world be as empty as mine should roles reverse.

It seems sad that my life has come to this,
If I end my self and my misery,
What will become of my Henry,

For my life revolves around him,
His mahogany colours shine,
His white blaze the gloss of polished onyx,
His eyes so loving and trusting.

For there is one who is so overjoyed to see my return,
One who fills my life with joy,
Someone who only ever agrees with me,
And doesn't moan at my going out,
Who only insists on my safe return.

Whether I'm drunk or sober,
Happy or sad,
Henry greets me at the door,
Wagging tail and slavering jowls,
Happy, excited and relieved to see me again.

But as for me,
What will I do when he leaves me.

June 10th 2004

Out of place, out of time

As I lay gazing out,
I watch the moon pass across the night sky,
Stars shine like diamonds in their own little world,
Wishing I was far from my life,
To a place where the sun of contentment burns my skin.

Caught in a twilight world,
Where Father Time outruns my mental image,
I mask with the trappings of younger years,
My mind and body keeping up,
Outlasting my juniors,
A boy of eighteen trapped in the body of my father.

Alas, my face shows my life,
Like an open book,
Trace for yourself the lines of sadness and joy,
Laughter, tears, accident or misadventure,
It gives away my age like a birthday badge,
Worn proudly by younger men,
With shame and embarrassment by older,
Cute works when you're young,

And hangs like chains of sin when approaching middle age,
At the speed of light unrelenting and harsh.

Though I try to outrun,
It gains on me with horrifying pace,
Soon to trample me and chew me up,
Spat out and wasted,
No longer able to hide,
No longer able to disguise,
Is it now time to face the truth.

As I sit surrounded by twenty-somethings,
Lights flash, bodies gyrate, drinks abound,
Rhythmic pounding of heavy bass lines crash,
Ripping through my brain,
Telling me my time has passed.

The neon sign above my head screams out my truth,
No longer Peter Pan in this Neverland,
Just an old pretender about to be revealed,
A bitter old soak is what I'm evolving to,

Can others see through my veneer,
Am I still able to hide my addiction,
A constant need to smooth out life,
With all its edges,
Sharp enough to lacerate my fragile dreams,
Leaving them tattered and torn at my feet,

Work in progress,
Or a write-off,

Not worth the time and effort to fix,
Give up, persevere,
Pack my bags and leave,
Or stay and fight,
Who am I.

I'm out of place, out of time.

7th August 2004

Where will I find her?

I search my horizons,
Everywhere I travel,
Where will she be?
Will I miss by a second?
An inch, how close is a near miss?

A wrong turn or declined invitation,
Or just place my trust in fate,
Should I just let it wash over me?
Or work against it,
Proactive reactive.

She is out there,
I can feel her and smell her perfume honeysuckle sweet,
Filling my mind with a beautiful image of perfection,
Filling my dreams with love and clouds of floating red silk,
Filling my ears with sweet soul music from a bygone age,
Filling my days with despair having not found her,
Patience is a virtue,
But not me.

But with impatience comes despair,
Do I reek of desperation?
Should I give an air of disinterest?
Or swallow my pride and make a move,
Never one to wear my heart on my sleeve,
Can my overeagerness be seen in my eyes,
A true gateway to my soul.

Oh to sleep to be with her again,
To touch my life without form or substance,
Like the drifting smoke from a gun,
Bullet to my broken heart,
Killing me over and over, night after night when I wake alone,
Image fragile, hang there a while till the alarm,
Jolts me back to an empty bed,
She dances through my sleep, I awake and she's gone,
I sleep again to no avail, just the DJ droning on,
Filling me with fury, smashing the clock,

Am I searching in the wrong places?
Lonely hearts and date line are not for me,
Am I looking for the right person?
The mirage of attractiveness,
Beer goggles,
Insanity to be caught up in fantasy,
Does the search keep going?
Or drive me closer to a loaded gun

Where will I find her?
Do we gaze at the same moon?

The same starry sky,
Wishing for each other,
Or is she just a dream.

10th August 2004

Gamble with the reaper

What's its attraction,
Slowly killing me from the inside,
With stealth unseen until too late,
Every time I light one it's a gamble,
Like a one-armed bandit, three black tumours,
Jackpot, a wooden overcoat,
No avalanche of jingling coins here,
Just one over each blank, staring and lifeless eye,
Never again to see a richly coloured sunset,
Reds, orange, deep blues and warming gold,
The world in all its glory,
Relinquished for five minutes of relief,
The enticing swirl of smoke,
The warming feel as it fills my lungs,
Bittersweet as anxiety passes into joy,
Bursting through my head like fireworks,
Relieving my craving if only for a while,
Nicotine monster abates once more,
Like a retreating sea at low tide,
Soon enough the sea will return to this beach,
As the silver smoke rises,

And burning embers with warming tones,
The rays of sunlight dance through the smoke,
Like lights in early evening fog,
They beam through the ever-growing cloud of deathly smoke,
But life is good again, I relish the beauty I see,
Everything is right with the world,
Much to the distain of others around me,
But which of us is the selfish one?
The packet glares at me in warning of horrors unimaginable,
Adverts show my future,
Tubes scars, long draw-out death,
Images that don't stick,
messages lost in cravings,
Do I listen, do I care,
With nicotine fingers grasping at my mind and soul,
Pulling me in to its clammy deathly grip,
Unable to pull free,
Convincing my mind and body it's right,
Habit, addiction, weakness, obsession,
I don't know?
who does?
No longer done to be hard or cool in a crowd,
Too old for that,
What is the fascination,
why do I do it,
Slow suicide for the terminal coward,
Like a bizarre game of Russian roulette,
It will get me, I have no doubt,
The chips are stacked against me,
There's no beating the house in this game,
Just chance to quit while ahead,
So here we go again,

Like the first one of the day smoke burns my mouth and lungs,
Just like a fine malt would,
Comforting smells of mellow tobacco,
Warnings forgotten,
Adverts disregarded,
Life is straight again,
Then as many before them discarded and forgotten,
As with me,
Is this my affinity with my crutch,
All that's left is ash, grey, brittle and lacking substance,
But unlike the phoenix I may never rise again,
Can I ever truly rise from the ashes of my life,
Or will I remain used up,
Stubbed and trampled,
But for now I will just gamble with the reaper.

12th August 2004

Jo-Jo

Here I sit,
Many years on,
Was I right?
Was I wrong?
Everything I have done to myself,
All life's curves and twists,
A roller coaster of misadventure that never ends,
I ponder my existence for what its worth,
All alone, no kith or kin,
I was happy with who I am,
Am I still?
Is life now worth its sacrifices?
Like an amputee,
I still feel her with me,
What have I become,
Not at all that I had planned,
Of mice and men I suppose,
Without my love,
Insomnia gets worse,
More waking hours to feel the loneliness,
Destroying me bit by bit,

I build my armour but she still gets through,
No matter what I do to repel the attacks of my memories,
Ones of happier times and sunnier days,
Full of laughter and smiles,
All now left is a band of gold,
Sad songs pang of my choices,
Right or wrong,
Who's to say, not I,
How many times can a heart be broken?
Like a labourer's hands,
My heart covered with calluses of rejection,
Not fit to give again,
Will I trust another to repair my life?
She's with him now,
Me with my beer,
Are we as happy as the faces we paint on?
To protect ourselves from the enemies at the gate,
Do we rue the day we parted,
I believe I do at times, sat in a darkened room,
Does she with her new life think of me?
Or am I just a fading photograph on the mantelpiece of her
memory,
Soul mate, confidant, best friend and lover,
Mother to my babies,
How do I start to replace,
The tracks of my tears are visible under my painted smile,
Keep them at arm's length,
No harm, no foul,
True love is like a narcotic,
Separation a never ending cycle of cold turkey,
No substitute ever compares to the high,
No replacement ever fills the void,

Left with a hole that can never be filled,
Surrounding myself with my life,
To protect me from the pain,
Sheltered from the heartbreak by my cheeky bravado,
So what becomes of us now?
Five lives damaged for the sake of what,
Change is as good as a rest,
Or is it,
And for whom?
Surely not me,
Or am I just being selfish,
But now it's gone,
Never to be reborn,
Take care of yourself,
And be happy, my Jo-Jo.

15th August 2004

Alcohol nights and hazy days

What must he be thinking,
My liver, that is,
For a decade or more,
Treated with respect,
For many years now bludgeoned,
Bathed, marinated and pickled,
A torrent of alcohol like Niagara Falls,
Spills down my throat with the urgency only alcoholics know,
Drowning out the screaming voices in my head,
Dulling life's pain and torment,
Three swift beers,
All-night parties,
All-day sessions,
Recall the last few years,
Not really,
Nothing clear or concise,
Just the groaning liver and kidneys the only indication of my
addiction,
One-way trip to the morgue,
But relief from my maddening mind,
Chance for one last party,

So much beer,
So little time,
It's no way to go,
A moment of clarity in a sea of mist,
Getting fewer the further I drift,
Darkness falls again,
Voices getting louder,
Losing my will to resist them,
Slowly driving me mad,
Destroying my mind,
Destroying me,
Anger rises,
Vision turning red,
Monsters scream inaudible nonsense,
Did he nudge me, what's his problem,
Gripping the glass,
Fingers and knuckles bled of colour,
Turning white, deep breaths,
Must calm my rage,
One swift shot, something hard,
Warming, calming, move on, have fun,
But is this life fun,
Or just a continuation,
Of my alcohol nights,
And hazy days.

19th August 2004

My Angel

Is this an angel entering my life,
A gift from the heavens to save me from my life,
Can she quell my demons,
Set me on the mysterious path to happiness,
What have I done to be so lucky,
Is it fate,
Or just my time,
Spending hours talking,
Voices floating to the heavens and back,
What wondrous things will happen from here,
But let's not fast-forward life,
Just enjoy each magical second of discovery,
Each hour of intimacy,
To kiss her warm skin, to feel her warm breath on mine,
To watch her sleep,
To touch her hair,
Am I to be so lucky,
Such ecstasy I am filled with when she is near,
Every fibre of my body humming with electricity,
Butterflies inside fluttering once more,
Feeling eighteen again,

Excitement buzzes through me just to feel like this,
First time, once in a lifetime,
every time she looks my way,
Numbing my eternal pain,
Giving myself up to her completely,
The way she walks,
Her eyes sparkle like stars when she smiles,
A love so strong my heart cannot bear,
To be away from her is pain in its most intense,
I can't breath,
Gasping for air like a fish floundering on damp sand,
She come to my rescue, returning me to the sea of her love,
Warm and comforting,
Passionate in full intensity,
Finding me, baring my soul to her completely,
What happened to my shield protecting my fragile heart,
Never to be breached till now,
One night together was all it took,
For her magic to melt away my resistance,
One night etched on my soul, it will forever remain,
Tattooed on my heart, showing me love exists,
My angel, my love, my life, my reason, my baby,
What has become of me,
As long as she is here with me, who cares,
Let our lives unfold together,
I'm here for her and she for me,
She is the one,
She is my angel.

12th November 2004

Alone again

Here I go again,
Sadness and regret,
Two old friends,
With them come alcohol and despair,
Why me, I ask myself,
With resounding silence my answer comes,
Echoing in the black emptiness,
Telling me it's no more than I deserve,
Trailing many broken hearts behind me,
Like a whistling black locomotive,
Disappearing into the night,
Making me feel what I have done to others,
It's no more than I should go through,
Sad songs and adverts scream at me,
Here you go again, it's your crushing payback,
For tortures done to others,
This time I thought it was for real,
Not for a fortnight,
This time I thought I had hit the jackpot,
Back to the bottom of a beer glass,
Comfortable and numbing,

The pain subsides till sunrise,
Then the pain returns again and not just to the heart,
This time I was in the zone,
This time I thought it was forever,
I was there for the first time in my life,
Clare is the one or was the one,
Never will I find another,
Never will I love again,
I never looked for love,
But it found me,
I should learn my lesson,
Shag and leave is the way,
But why did she make me feel so different,
Why did I let her in,
She found her way through my shield,
And there she will stay,
Burnt into my heart with a searing pain,
I don't comprehend how I fell so hard,
But alas, I did,
But here I sit,
Alone again, naturally.

13th November 2004

Age concern

Age,
Young or old,
What's the point in counting?
Another year older,
Body showing signs,
Mind pretending in its immaturity,
Twenty-one to thirty-seven,
What's the difference,
Does it make us less happy?
Old Father Time pushes along,
Unforgiving and relentless,
The stigma of ever-increasing numbers on birthday cards,
The stench it gives off giving away your pretence,
I am no different than in years gone by,
A little wiser maybe,
Then again maybe not,
Mellowing to autumn years,
Slower than my peers,
In this winter of my discontent,
Clouded by my rose-tinted glasses of youth,
Or just my stubborn ferocity to ignore my pending middle age,

I live as my life,
In reverse to the norm,
Getting younger and more reckless as time slips away,
Closer to forty,
The age of my impending doom,
Once again ready to embrace the reaper,
We crumble as many times before,
I will once again taunt him to do his worst,
Beckoning on the deathly grip and cold earth,
Or have I been dead for years,
Just your kiss sparking animation back,
Heart jumps, stomach tingles just from your glance,
The only thing that has been right in my lifetime,
But alas, as a new toy at Christmas,
Played with till bored,
Returned to my box cold and lonely,
Assigned to a shelf of dust and dark,
Waiting to be turned on again,
Till then empty glances and meaningless nights,
The combination still to be sought,
Looking for the glove still yet to fit my hand,
Let's not wait too long,
Time ticks away,
Age rises,
Though it's not my concern,
Yours is the age concern.

15th November 2004

Love is

What is love,
love is everything, nothing, pain, pleasure, torment and ecstasy,
Love is the tingle of excitement,
The terror of rejection,
Love is the sublime feelings of exquisite joy,
The questioning of trust and honesty,
Love is the warm glow of December log fires,
The tangible fear of loneliness,
Love is complete understanding,
The pain from a bitter broken heart,
Love is the anguish of separated moments,
The destruction of bridges built,
Love is the recollection of happier times past and those to
come,
The shattered memories at your feet of life lost,
Love is the wonder of stolen moments,
The emptiness of singleness,
Love is the all-consuming adoration of beauty,
The pang of regret to see another in your place,
Love is the pleasure in its most extreme,
The extreme pain of love and love lost,

We crave it like drugs,
We are all burned by its furious light,
Its intensity we love and are loved intensely,
Will it last,
Or burn out like an exploding star,
The like to be never seen again,
Just the stabbing memory of what once was,
And if in luck we may see the like again,
The pain returns once more,
And the search goes on,
Love is.........love.

30th November 2004

In retreat

My deathly serpent was ever once growing,
Up through my soul,
Choking at my spine,
Making me twitch and contort,
Like a puppet at his master's request,
Slithering up into my brain,
Changing who I am and want to be,
Encircling my mind,
Constricting, squeezing me out,
Removing me from myself,
Extracting my personality,
In view of others,
In view of my own self-opinion,
Who am I becoming?
Who am I?
But wait,
Who is this coming in to my world?
A remedy or cure,
Maybe an angel to save me,
Or help me save myself,
Not like a movie romance,

But still the serpent is in retreat,
I return slowly to myself,
Coming back from this solitary hell,
Don't let me go,
Back to that place,
Cold and dark,
Demons howl and scream,
Not anywhere you want to be,
But should she leave I will return,
And willingly so, just one mouthful of sweet nectar,
Why can't I be stronger?
The will to resist is all I need,
Would she send me back if she knew,
It's not fair to keep her with me,
Just to avoid my personal hell,
Should I let her fly free from the cage that entraps her?
Free her beauty and warmth back to the sunnier world she
inhabits,
Or does she need me just as much,
Are we saving each other from our own nightmares?
Our own personal serpents,
But with mine retreating day by day,
Another takes its place,
Green eyes glowing in the dark,
It grips my soul with an icy hand,
Making my fears grow,
Neither hell nor high water,
I barely get by being me,
No added pressures,
But I need to be in this place,
Just substituting one demon for another,
Which do I prefer?

Which will I succumb too completely?
I will have to wait in ever-growing feeling of doom,
Just a bitter old soak,
Never to change,
Never wanting to,
Do I get off on depression?
Is this my kick?
Do I not want to succeed?
Is it a relentless fear of being happy?
I could be this time,
If I really tried,
I do love,
And need to be loved,
The cloak she hides behind,
Reminiscent of mine,
Keeping the world of hurt away,
Non-discriminating of good and bad,
Nice or nasty,
How can I show my intentions to be good?
In a childlike honesty,
Reborn in virginity of white silk,
Embraced like the first sunrise,
But such is life in mistrust and dishonesty,
To be hurt is commonplace,
To live in life is to live in pain,
Still my serpent is in retreat.

30th November 2004

Three fifty a.m.

Music on the stereo,
Cigarette butts in the ashtray,
Empty beer cans strewn,
Whisky glass half empty,
Or half full,
Numbing of my mind and senses,
I sit alone and all the signs show,
Insomnia returns,
My love sleeps away from me,
And has been for many hours,
My mind slurs,
Vision wavers,
But yet sleep still evades me,
Depression waits at the door,
At least until the lights go out,
Nine minutes to four,
The clock ticks away more slowly, arms stand still,
Half a can left,
Words scream around my head and fall onto the page,
All at once realising life will change come sunrise,
About to be left again,

If only you could see how much I love you,
And want to protect you from harm,
To show you true happiness,
To give you the moon and stars,
To give you the universe you deserve,
All the riches that life in happiness has to offer you,
Never to break your heart or hurt you,
As many before,
You're my goddess to be worshipped and revered,
To save you, to save me,
Time to sleep,
I don't want to wake in case I am in torment again,
Let me sleep forever, still in love and loved,
To die happy is my wish,
Morbid thoughts hammer my tired mind,
As darkness doesn't get any lighter,
What lurks in the dark is just fear,
My fear rises that come morning I may wake,
And face the afternoon single again,
Need to sleep,
Five past four and it's time,
Close my eyes,
Nightmares await me,
Laughing in the dark,
With pure insanity,
Ten past four and goodnight.

30th November 2005

Clare

Oh how that name resounds through my mind,
Butterflies flutter on wings of silk,
every time she looks my way,
Her soft brown hair the colour of rich mahogany,
It shines like gold catching the early morning sun,
Like beams dancing through fields of autumn wheat,
Her eyes with the sparkle of winter stars,
Her sweet smile shows me what lies beneath her veneer,
She makes me feel eighteen again, going through my first crush,
To touch her soft skin,
To feel her soft sensuous touch on me,
To smell her sweet perfume,
I wait for her,
To see her, time passes slower tick by tick,
I wait as my patience starts to ebb,
Eager to see my love,
For it's her who makes me whole again,
To be in love with Clare,
As refreshing as summer rain before a storm,
Electricity hums through the atmosphere,
We love and are loved,

Can it last forever,
life is clear once more,
It lightens up my life like a spring morning,
But soon to end I'm sure,
Will fate play its hand again,
To free her once more,
Back to the heavens,
Am I worthy to posses such a beauty,
You can't love until you learn to love yourself,
To love me must be mad,
Do I love,
Can I love,
Christmas again will the curse return,
Without a doubt,
To be single again,
Like an unwanted toy,
Waiting to be returned,
But to where,
Singleness and unhappiness,
It's just my way,
To linger in the twilight world of alcohol,
Oh my love lost,
Farewell to my love,
Good bye Clare.

25th December 2004

Drink

What is this monster I see before me?
Cloaked in its invisible shield of glass,
Inanimate but totally controlling,
From its first warming sip,
To its last dribbling effects,
I like how she makes me feel,
But hate the way she makes me,
Sane to goon in six shots,
Coherent to unintelligible in ten,
Sociable to antisocial in many more,
Tricks to make you last longer,
Longer you last maximises the carnage,
Body gives up, mind carries on,
Needing, lusting and gagging,
Mind and body swim and slow,
Eyes flicker, can they tell,
Once more in a bad place,
Help me please,
Well maybe not,
Comforting in its unknown effect,
Believing in a top drunk,

A drunk is a drunk,
A pound is a pound,
No matter how you slice it,
It is what it is,
Call a spade a spade,
A rose by any other name,
What's your poison?
Certain death in prolonged agony,
Is that with ice and a slice sir?
Unattractive,
Why would life play out this way?
Is it controlled or controlling?
Pleasure or pain,
Will a destructive night destroy me?
Will I destroy this bottle?
Or be bottled trying to destroy,
Adverts of attractive people,
Playing at fun on this devil,
Are they attractive after?
Do they attract us?
Such shallow tricks,
Of course they do,
We are the army of alcoholics paying for these adverts,
One leg on the wagon,
Or just knowing the path its on,
Oh sod it, let's get pissed,
We can get the next one,
Drink, get drunk, fall over, what problem,
Eyes bulge as I stay silent,
Keeping count, count keeping,
Liver shrinks and kidneys howl as my head shudders,
Not remembering,

Three years lost,
Life ticks away,
Almost dead or just fucked up,
The only absolute truth is death.

26th December 2004

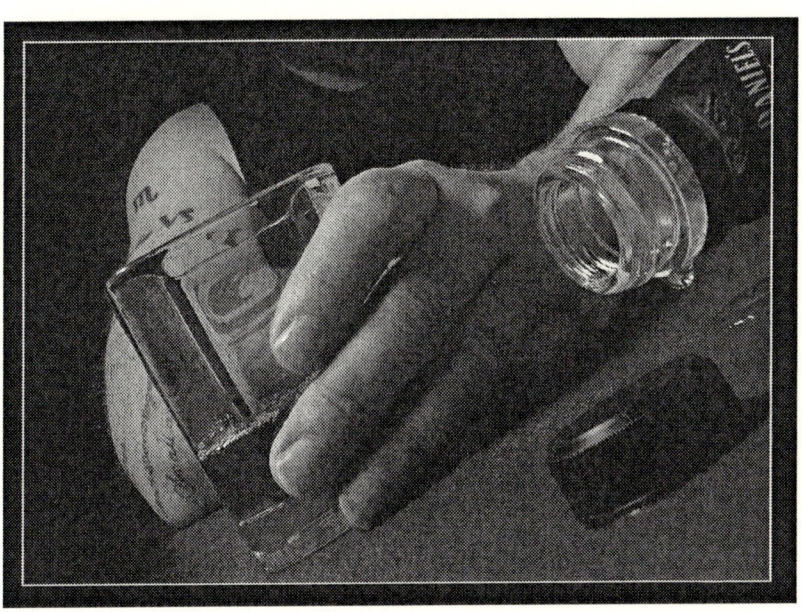

Short-term love

Love in its most magnificent,
Beautiful, passionate, erotically stirring the innermost parts of
being,
Mental, physical, totally engulfing like fire,
Burning and consuming me from inside out,
But cherish every moment while it lasts I must,
Not to squander a second of it,
A short-term love that cannot hope to last,
No longer everlasting in this disposable society,
Almost as with time you get less for your money,
They storm into your life,
Turning it inside out as they rage through,
Turning your emotions into tornadoes,
Your love into tsunamis to drown your will to resist,
Leaving you uncontrollably happy,
But as the hurricane it blows out just as fast,
Leaving behind torn and tattered effects,
That once used to be your life,
Passing lovers leaving behind a bleak landscape that once was
your heart,
All that's left is emptiness and memories,

But like the obsessive you crave more,
One night of love,
One evening of ecstasy,
One last chance to kiss her lips,
To feel her skin and touch her hair or smell her sweet scent,
Their love as transient as the seasons,
But short-lived,
The only outcome for such intensity,
A firework display never forgotten,
Time spent healing is all-consuming,
More baggage to manhandle to the next season,
Heavier than Marley's chains of sin,
Another ballad to play on your mind,
Tears start to sting these eyes which once held such beauty,
Do I trigger this in them,
My need for love and loss,
Is my capacity for love short-lived,
Is it the pain which fuels my life,
Or just the scars of modern love,
The McDonald's culture seeping into life,
It ain't over till the fat lady sings,
Will she fall silent this time.

28th December 2004

But alas, to lose again

Where will I find her,
By surprise long before I knew her,
A night not to be forgotten,
Right through the early hours,
till sunrise and I'm thirty-seven,
Leaving me to choose between two,
But there's no doubt as to who will win,
I dilly and dally to break a heart,
But break it I must,
Leading me to chose one who will ultimately break mine,
But it's a choice I make with a willing joy,
Knowing it can't last,
Wishing it would,
An impossible love,
Unable to resist,
As with Adam and the apple I readily bite,
To lead me to an uncertain world,
But now at an unhappy end I look back,
In retrospect I wouldn't change,
I enjoy the memories of us,
Stolen afternoons in bars,

Wandering the shops arm in arm,
Public affection and ecstasy,
Sharing a bed, stories and life,
Planning trips never to be taken,
Now my life as quiet as before,
A longing heart yearns to turn back time,
A sensible mind enjoying my reflections,
The spring was full of wonder and surprise,
New to the touch, exploring the beautiful new dawn,
My mind and body loving the feeling of spiritual rebirth,
A summer spent basking in her warmth,
Touched by the words she sent to me,
Tear of joy tremble behind my eyes,
Awaiting the moment to tumble down my cheeks,
Trying to be seen but never to fall,
The cold chill of November banished from me,
For the first time in many years I'm alive,
Christmas approaches at speed,
Trees and presents bought,
Bows and coloured paper beckon,
My personal Scrooge locked away,
No bah humbug for me,
We await the day in childlike anticipation,
Behind me autumn approaches like a silent assassin,
To kill my lover's love for me,
I, Mr Mistrust, bound in my lover's eyes and words,
Too preoccupied to notice my impending doom,
The autumn chill grabs me as her embers wane,
Her eyes begin to cool,
Her love and lust for me die as winter sets in,
Images of what was to be a happier day,
Full of gifts and love,

Shatter like ice around my feet,
Leaving me to recollect,
Alone and silent, just the pop of another can is perceptible,
But I thank the mysterious power that bought her to me,
No regrets or tears,
Just leaving me a warm place in my mind for her,
A place she will live forever,
But now's the time to move on in substance,
To find a new,
In the unfolding, yet-to-be future,
But in the tangible spirit of history of Christmas past,
May we dance forever in never ending love.

28th December 2004

Yesterday I was loved

Yesterday,
As long ago as it was,
I was loved,
Messages in an eternal memory show this to be true,
As my mind's picture starts to flicker and fade,
Oh and how I was loved,
Best of love, best of life,
Sixty days in full spectrum.
With no regrets to what I threw away,
More than I deserve was my reward,
Never to forget,
But love is never eternal,
As unfortunate as it now appears,
Once more in my single cell,
Wishing for the first time,
In a bar lighting up a dull world,
A birthday present to cherish,
Just in her presence, nothing tangible to unwrap,
But later to unwrap her soft and warm,
To lose her is pain at any time of the year,
But Christmas Day's not fair,

Winded and speechless,
Just one last day if I had my choice,
It would have been this one,
But now on Boxing Day,
Just me, José, salt and lemon,
Wishing for a time machine,
To live over again,
Like a Christmas rerun,
Once, twice, maybe live forever in yesterday,
Even with a gun to my head I would not deny,
Her warmth behind her cloak was mine alone to see,
No one allowed to get close,
A pussycat in a lion's coat,
We could have been contenders for love everlasting,
But alas, I wasn't to be,
What we had so spectacular,
Sad to let it go,
But let it go we must,
Never again to see her face come Auld Lang Syne,
We will raise a glass from miles away,
Separated by countryside and borders,
And her need for personal space,
So leave me as you found me,
Empty just one more scar,
But for now I reminisce,
And if only for a little while,
Yesterday I was loved.

30th December 2004

New Year

So here it is,
It's crept round with its usual stealth,
New Year once more,
Soon to be,
Hello to the new,
Goodbye to the old,
What surprises to bring,
Just wait and see,
But reflect on the past,
We just can't help,
Farewell to those who have past,
Hoping to replace with new,
As for me,
Alas, alone again,
Surrounded by couples all happy in love,
If only for the silly season,
Cracks patched over by food and booze,
As for my love,
It died a week ago,
With the slamming of a door,
Now just me and the dog again,

Same as last few years past,
A habit I must break,
If only for my sanity,
So I sit and reflect on what's just passed,
And what is to come,
So just for now,
Eat, drink and make merry,
Happy New Year to you all,
And to all a good year.

31st December 2004

My life in progress

Father,
Husband,
Chef,
Alcoholic,
Which am I now,
I live my life as a work in progress,
Am I what I want,
I'm not sure,
Am I who I can be,
Absolutely not,
I am a work in progress,
Am I who people want me to be,
Who cares,
Do I love myself,
Absolutely not,
How can anyone love this image before them,
Is this a vicious circle I find myself in,
Being drunk because I'm not loved,
Or not being loved because I drink,
But to be sober would kill me,
But not to be loved is killing me,

Who can believe my life is in progress,
When I can't say my own name,
But I remember leaving the pub,
that's progress,
Sober to hang from a beam,
Dead and lifeless,
Is that progress,
Should I die, who would shed a tear,
just a relief from this hell on earth,
Loving, loosing, drinking,
I'm me, not fixed, just me,
What you see is what you get,
No more,
No less,
In progress is what I am,
Nothing special,
Just take me,
And make me,
I am a life in progress.

9th January 2005

I remember Sunday

Tense and nervous,
Stomach turning to knots,
Roller coaster innards,
But to break a heart must be done,
Need to be single again by Sunday,
Sunday with my newfound love,
Well, love-to-be,
Hit between the eyes,
Magical thunderbolt,
Surely only in films,
But how badly does my old love take it,
Worse than can be imagined,
But I would sit through an eternity of this,
Just for the memory of that Sunday,
A Sunday to make me love every Sunday,
A Sunday to love every Sunday that ever was,
And I hate Sundays,
As any atheist would,
As a child it was bath night,
The scent of freshly washed sheets would haunt my life,

School the next day,
The night my wife strayed,
The night my grandfather died,
I hate Sundays with a passion,
Now I work them,
I hate them even more,
But after that Sunday I can only love them,
Oh to live that day forever,
that's my heaven,
In bed with my lover till midday,
Soft, tender, loving and sexy,
So to begin eight weeks of rapture,
Now I love Sundays,
Never wanting to forget the feelings over lunch,
No, watching her get ready,
To spend time,
New and unknowing,
Even now,
I remember and it's so sweet,
Nectar of the gods,
Now left in squalor and dirt,
Wind blows through the broken window,
Rain drips on the carpet with the repetitive sound of a leaking tap,
Single two weeks,
Now the new year nine days old,
I still remember,
Pub lunches,
Her smell,
The way she looked,
And looked at me,
Just to be there again,

Adoring and to be adored,
I still remember Sunday.

9th January 2005

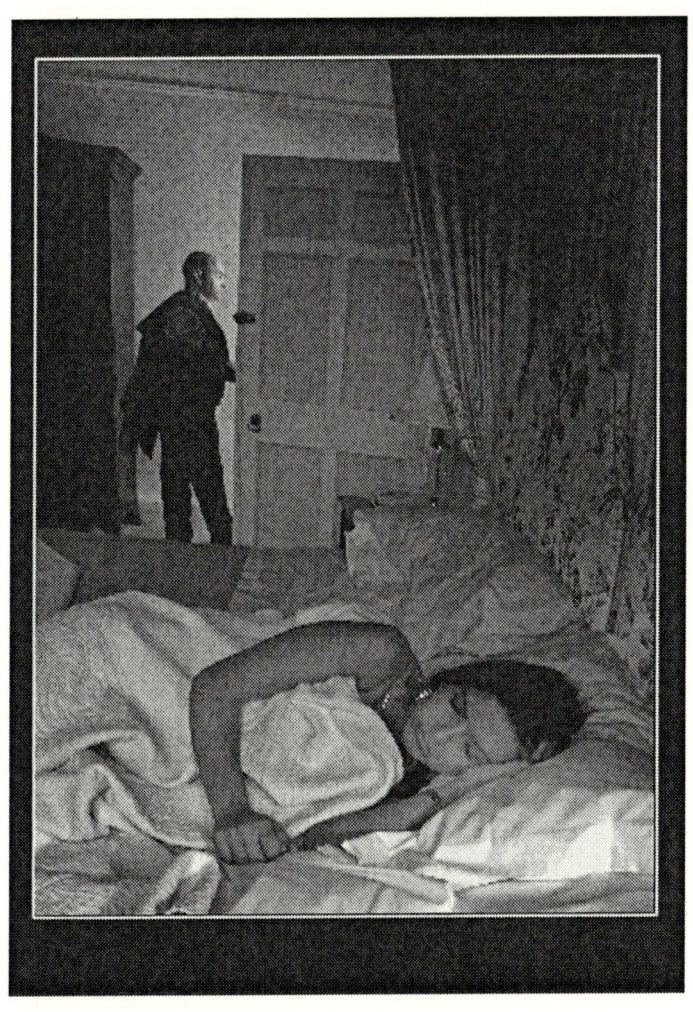

Ghosts of future and past

Here I sit, 2047,
Eighty years young,
Senile, dribbling and stinking of piss,
A faded second-hand chair coming away at the seams,
Gravy splashes and greasy mark,
Help to frame a picture of a more sorry sight,
Lost and away in memories,
All I have left to show for four score years,
No one visits or calls,
All bridges burnt long before,
Like an army in retreat, no way back,
My life ends as it began,
In a troubled council flat,
On a troubled estate,
In fear I would live,
If my possessions were of any value,
To anyone but me,
The only gold I posses are my golden memories of better
times,
Arthritis burns my hands,
Fading eyes making my reminiscences brighter,

Behind my eyes is where I now exist,
But this is many years from now,
Only halfway along my journey,
This view doesn't have to be,
Or is it set and waiting for me to arrive,
Can I change this ending to my existence?
Am I my own script writer?
My days of womanising and drinking,
In full swing as I sit here and type,
But I don't always cause the hurt,
I have been hurt,
And have lost, not always thrown,
My woman is out there waiting somewhere,
Of that I'm sure,
My reward and pot of gold at the end of the rainbow,
But as with the horizon it remains elusive,
Will I make the same mistakes when I catch her?
In triumph of catching the rare and beautiful butterfly,
Will I display her?
Killing her,
To lose her,
Or will I let her fly free in confidence of her return to me,
Filling my life with colour and warmth,
But for now I look for that special sign,
Leading me to her vibrance,
Leading me to her light,
But as daylight fades on another January day,
I sit and slumber,
Ghostly images haunt my sleeping hours,
Haunted by that chair,
Mahogany legs hanging from its green mass,
Chasing me through my sleep,

In chilling shades of grey I now dream,
All the colours bled away,
Living in a perpetual winter,
By then it will be too late,
No life left to share,
Where are you,
Rescue me from this nightmare,
Help me, let it never be,
Never be me,
My turn will come,
Of that I'm sure.

17th January 2005

A place like home

There's no place like home,
And this is nowhere like home,
Stale smoke and sticky tables,
Rancid smell of yeasty beer and pre-packed food,
But this is home now,
This can't have happened to me,
Looking for clues in sad songs on the jukebox,
In the eyes of the others along the bar,
My fellow bar flies with their own sad stories,
True or false they stick to them,
Getting worse further down the line you go,
Is this the course of my degeneration?
One-way ticket to Waterloo Bridge,
And cocktails in vivid purple with less American dry,
My mind snapped back to now by the last order bell,
That time already, do I need a takeout?
Thinking through my swimming mind,
Well, while I do, a pint and a chaser please,
Down the chaser with the kick of a mule,
Warming my icy soul,
But doesn't chase the pain away,

Two more shots to keep the cold out, I lie,
But to whom,
Eleven twenty and I'm woken by the shout,
Drink up, gentlemen, please,
Ain't you got homes to go to,
Well I have and I drift back,
To a time,
House, car, two point three children, Mr Average,
But they were good times,
In the summer of my life,
But now outside the winter wind howls,
Trees sway against the night,
Body screams a little less abuse,
Insomnia haunts my nights,
Alcohol haunts my days,
Monsters scream twenty-four/seven,
Ears ring, heart yearns and mind swims in perpetual daze,
What's dreaming?
What's real?
The cycle of love and love lost in vicious intent,
Kills me a little more each time,
Smoke one more nail for my beckoning coffin,
Pick up my coat,
Pulled up tight against the night air,
The only sign of life is my warm breath,
Grey and lifeless on the cold night air,
Footsteps echo,
The army of drunks all over this land,
Trudging the way home in a musicless dance,
The closing time dance natural and never taught,
For me my door calls and emptiness howls,
From within a shadow of my past flickers,

Alas, just wisps of breath and shading of drink,
My footsteps fall on carpetless floors and ring out,
Open the fridge but not for food,
Children's laughter no longer lights the dark corners,
No warm and soft lover to chase away my torment,
If this is hell give me back my heaven,
Praised and never taken for granted again,
If I'm taken before I wake, thank god,
If not then why,
Body tired from living this life,
To wake is to return,
Each day a carbon of the last,
All that changes is the volume of consumption,
To begin again and never to learn,
A pint and a chaser,
bar steward,
Click my heels but still I remain,
No it ain't nothing like home.

18th January 2005

Don't break my heart

Here I am,
Fragile in feeling,
Not too big to cry,
Here's my heart,
Exposed and real,
No pretence to be found here,
I am a man,
But don't be fooled by my tough appearance,
I have feeling too,
Don't tar me with the same brush,
As others before,
For those I apologise,
But I am not them,
And they not me,
Sex I have had in plenty,
Loved only twice,
Give me the chance, I have been waiting,
The brusque bravado is my shield to protect me,
To shield my tender heart from hurt that always follows,
Inside me a small child cowers in the corner,
Just like the willow I have wept,

Unsure and afraid,
Release the child from the prison he finds himself in,
Free me from the pain with which I have been inflicted,
And which I now inflict,
Not proud of my past,
But never wishing to change or forget,
As now mid-life leaps at me with surprise,
I find my heart still in the possession of one,
Who threw me away many years since,
Show me what I miss and have been missing,
Make me, don't break me,
Free me from my new masters,
In whose grip I am lost forever,
Help me love the sunrise in your arms,
And starlight in your love,
Protect me from the venom of my demons,
Like clay in your hands I can be formed,
Or broken and discarded,
Discover me as an artist discovers his fresh canvas,
Don't distrust me because I have miles on the clock,
As virginal as in the beginning,
Here's my heart, take it,
Make it,
Just please don't break it.

28th January 2005

Emerald City

The tornado disrupting and powerful,
Ripping its way through,
Removing me from my life,
Discarding me dazed and confused into this bizarre dream,
But surely the only emerald for me,
Is the green grass above me,
Encased in concrete of gloom it slows my journey,
No magical scarlet shoes for me,
But for now the world of dreams and nightmares,
Journeying the Yellow Brick Road to my Emerald City,
I find no comfort in my surroundings or friends,
The bizarre and grotesque caricature I have become,
Drawn by one who see beyond my eyes,
As different to me as can be possible,
The Jeckel and Hyde effects of substance abuse,
Effects last longer till almost engulfed,
Its sharp talons in my flesh,
Searing pain tearing through my soul and mind,
Ripping me apart from inside out,
Pain darts through my heart and soul,
Soon to be lost forever in purposelessness,
Killing the pain in the only way I know,

Vision through blurring eyes set on my goals ahead,
My addictions dragging me back,
Arms from below pulling me back down,
Dark swirling mist behind me beckons me back,
Sweet images before me of carefree days and careless nights,
Sunny horizons clear and sharp calling me on,
Promising intent of a younger me,
To be loved and adored with a purpose once more,
Will I get there in this life or the next,
Will the wonderful wizard help me should I get there,
Pushing myself to escape,
Wanting to sit alone,
Unsure of me,
Unsure of life,
Unsure if I want to change,
Or just sit and decompose,
Crying through the night,
Screaming through the day,
Let me be free from myself,
Free me from my life,
Free me from the bondage of being,
Let me run to my destiny,
Never getting any closer,
Just further away each day,
Monsters in the mist winning me over,
Shall I ever see the Emerald City in this lifetime,
Shall I get to give my wishes to the wizard,
No patience left,
Just anger and hatred,
Let me be free again.

30th January 2005

77

Am I whom I portray?

Here I am, last door on the left,
Habitual resident of the heartbreak hotel,
Time weighs heavy on my hands,
Left to ponder my own shortcomings,
Looking for the yin to my yang,
The gentle goat searching for his sign,
Yet is life controlled by the stars,
Or the point of my birth,
Are my characteristics set by my time of arrival?
Back to the present and what I need to do,
When I look in the mirror I see me reflected back,
What do you see?
Am I the only one who can see who I am?
My heart on my sleeve,
The image I portray for my protection,
Far removed from the lost soul that I am,
Hiding from the world around me and the hurting it offers,
Within maybe too far gone for rescue,
In my façade time to call a halt,
Permanent markings accentuating my fearsome exterior,

The warmth of my heart blotted out by clouds of loathing,
Like sunshine on a stormy August day,
In a turbulent world of trepidation I live,
Can't show me without love,
Or find love without revealing,
Too long in the tooth to change?
Too young to learn by my mistakes?
For arrogance read panic,
For immodesty read self-effacing,
I wear my external mask as a warrior wears his armour,
The suit comes off when alone,
When all at once my feelings appear on the screen,
Fastened up when on show,
Will these words be my only evidence in my defence?
Or will I give way under the pressure of examination,
Have I always been afraid to show my vulnerability?
Have people seen glimpses of me,
Is my only crime the fear of rejection?
Can we ever trust others to handle our inner selves?
With the care we would handle theirs,
Are we all guilty of thoughtlessness?
But in my protection comes conflict,
My mind longs to be alone,
My heart yearns to be coupled,
Split in two by indecision,
Ending in one-night stands,
Four-week flings,
Will this ever end or end up ended,
If I'm to end like this, is it fair,
Have I been fair for it to end any other way,
So here I sit,

Lost in a sea of desolation,
The flame of the lighthouse torch long since extinguished,
Am I whom I portray?
Who am I?
What do I portray?

28th March 2005

While we wait

I had what I always wanted,
Then I lost it,
But I will wait till she returns,
She may decide not to,
But still I wait,
Meanwhile I will lose control,
I will drink,
Chase women,
Live the bachelor life and all that it brings,
And still I wait,
I will have my fun,
Or so it seems through goggles of beer,
But still I wait,
Soul crippled and emotions tangled,
Tears burn and smart behind these eyes,
But still I wait,
Soon she will see sense,
No more to see her sparkle,
My life's sky with an absence of stars,
The twinkle in her baby blues no longer lights it up,

The sunrise of her smile no longer lights my days,
But still I wait,
My heart drops to my shoes,
Her laughter no longer lifts it,
Once was like a helium balloon,
Released it would float free,
Up to the heavens chasing rainbows across her smile,
But still I wait,
Surely she can't resist me,
And still I wait,
No way it can be over forever,
Never more to swim in her eyes,
Or watch sunlight dance in her hair,
Terrible visions of my life stretch out before me,
But still I wait,
This can have no happy ending,
No once upon a time bedtime story,
Why do I wait?
Pride?
Pissed that away long ago,
Fear?
Not with this level of alcohol,
Do I still find this life fun?
But to sleep now,
Just to see her in my dreams,
Happier days set in golden sepia tones,
But still I wait,
Why do I wait?
Don't ask, I don't have the answers,
So till later,
I wait and in waiting I dream,

To be with my first and only love,
But still I wait,
Forever in waiting,
I will wait.

30th March 2005

To realise my demons

Am I the demon I try to outrun,
Is it myself I'm running from,
I fear that now at harvesting I find I reap what I have sown,
As I demonise one life after another,
Not taking the weight of this burden on my shoulders,
Not sharing the responsibilities of failure,
As my own demon I seek only to destroy,
And in destruction is my only joy,
Is it all to keep love and reality at arm's length?
To keep me safe from hurting,
I stay running,
If just for my sanity,
Never again to suffer or cause suffering,
Pound in the jukebox,
Elvis again,
Reminiscing over better times,
Of blossom falling in late spring,
Like the confetti of our August day,
Was your intention to destroy me?
Did you wish for this bitter end?

I wished my whole life on shooting stars,
Did it not work for me?
Asking you back,
You didn't answer,
Loving me as a friend,
I hear your name, but only on the wind,
My heart still loves,
But you still posses it,
Let me be free to shake off this hell I am in,
The twilight world of fear and loathing,
Leave me free from these chains that bind me,
To no longer live in emotional bondage,
But until my emancipation just the insanity of echoes
A swirling mist of squealing vultures,
Waiting for my demise to devour me,
I sit in the darkness with time to ponder,
And watch myself from afar,
Making the same mistakes,
Cringing as I do over and over again,
Let me be who I can be and want to be,
Leave me free to feel these butterflies inside once more,
But for now I'm imprisoned outside looking in,
Others free to enjoy this life bestowed on them,
As for me,
On the periphery of a greater life,
Waiting for my chance to hop on,
Will this carousel ever come to a stop for me?
Or will I have to wait in this eternal queue,
Don't leave me to be your slave,
Until it's too late and buried in my grave,
To grow old and decay,
Does my demon show to others,

Through my aura,
Till the day I'm free from this life,
I will forever be a demon and demonise.

15th May 2005

Mr Hyde to resurface

What is this vision I see before me,
An angel bathed in golden light,
An image of beauty or my mind playing tricks,
A mirage in my desert of destiny,
Or a genuine oasis in which to replenish my strength,
Oh please let her be real,
For it's she who lights my darkened soul,
It's she who resonates light to the moon and stars,
Makes the sun rise and set,
She returns the colour back to my life,
And the stars back to my night,
Returns my body back to summer,
My mind released from winter into joys of spring,
A smile so sweet it could melt the hardest of hearts,
Eyes in which to lose yourself completely,
Once seen, never to be forgotten,
Hair shimmers like gold on a riverbed,
Life's colour comes back with a shock to my mind,
Leaving me stunned,
Unable to breathe,
Grass greener than emeralds,
Sun brighter and warmer on my skin,

Stars shimmer like diamonds,
Jealous to be outshone by her eyes,
Trees sway silently to the music of life once more,
I hear the chains of bondage break and fall from my heart,
A curse once cast long ago now broken,
Leaving me free to discover life with the zest of a child,
My cautious mind, wary mind,
My exuberant heart carefree,
But we have been here before,
Haven't we,
Past forgotten,
Future embraced,
Pain and regret left behind,
For the time being at least,
But the curse returns,
Eight weeks to the day,
No sooner,
No later,
Should I have forewarned you?
If I was only to steal from you,
I could not touch the tenderness inside,
And now I feel him rising,
To return once more,
Under all this pleasure a voice screams in the night,
Stay away from me,
This can only end in your hurt,
You deserve to be with one other than me,
Mr Hyde returns to break a heart and destroy,
What's wrong with me, I cannot tell?
Try to fix but to no avail.

2nd June 2005

My wish

Holidays full of fun,
Nights spent loving and close,
our days full of friends and love,
A life spent loving and keeping,
Where did we go wrong?
Where did I go wrong?
Where did we go?
Were did our love go,
Somewhere along life's journey,
We lost ourselves,
Why did we let it happen?
Why did we let go,
Neither of us wanted,
Or needed,
This travesty to happen,
A life made of mistakes since,
We live silently in misery,
Never wanting to tell the truth,
Never letting our true faces show,
How long must we pursue these false lives?
In silence we live,
In silence we may die,

Our feelings must remain,
We may deny,
We may protest,
And live a life of painted smiles,
But our souls know where they should be,
Our souls know we should be together,
To live till infinity,
One must bury the other,
Later rather than sooner,
As heartbreak kills either,
Do we both live lonely and unfulfilled,
Or do I just get off on my own self-importance,
One morning I may awake from this terrible nightmare,
And thank god it's just a dream,
But alas, today I wake alone,
It still remains,
the biggest sin since Adam and Eve,
The apple we did not bite,
But pay a similar price,
Thrown from paradise by our own wishes,
Now wandering in exile,
Our own demons to exorcise,
Never our paths to cross again,
Summers spent in love,
Winters spent inside,
Love grown and died,
But for my wish,
Would be to turn back time,
To summers spent in love,
And that is my wish.

3rd July 2005

A message from you

As I lay in this darkened room,
Drifting in and out of wakening,
Sam Cooke's harmonious tones floating through the two a.m. air,
Comforting songs of love and loss,
A message from you reawakens my past hurt,
Ghosts of past nights in your arms torment my dreams,
Mental tattoos dance and drift before my eyes when I wake,
A room that smells of ageing tobacco and dog,
This is what you left me with,
Your love a scar on my heart,
My joy decayed and poisonous to my soul,
Another cigarette,
Another glass of wine,
But the haunting still remains,
A wound that may never heal,
A life I can't leave behind,
A body ready to fall,
A mind that no longer cares,
To put this life behind is no shame,
All that remains are faded photographs,
And mentions in despatches,
Do I linger on your mind as you do mine?
Pinocchio to your Geppetto,

It's been too hard living,
But I'm not afraid to die,
I tell those who will listen,
That it can't come soon enough for me,
Or am I just kidding myself and others,
Alcohol and nicotine pushing me further,
The water of life needing to be refilled,
But only by those who do not want to drink from the well,
I still love you as I did then,
If I am to tell you, would you laugh in my face?
As I sit contemplating my life,
Another glass of wine for my life's novel,
And as I sit back looking over my writing,
I realise it was you,
You were my muse,
You touched me so deeply,
An arrow to my heart never to be removed,
Shrapnel burrowing deeper,
Searing into my flesh,
Contaminating my body never to recover,
It buries itself, shifting and burning,
Afflicted with love for you,
Our destinies on separate paths,
On my headstone to read,
To Clare,
My joy,
My pain,
My love,
My muse,
Caused just by a message from you.

6th July 2005

Last orders

To sell my soul for one last drink,
Before the darkness comes to take me away forever,
The spirit-taking bartender looms at the end of my universe,
My time has come to leave this stool,
One last time,
One last round,
Can you spare me the time,
One last drink,
For the eternal road,
Which queue do I join?
Up or down,
Next drink in purgatory?
A round with St. Peter and the choir eternal,
The barman in his black cloak edges along the bar,
He rings the bell,
Every step he encroaches,
Toward my impending end,
No chance for a lock-in,
Just to see one last sunset,
Will it be the perfect end to avoid the morning after,
How did I go, I think?

As my liver implodes and kidneys burst,
My own demon finally got his will,
My demise has always been written,
Just avoided the signs,
Thought it would be my lungs,
How silly do I now feel?
What's my legacy?
What mark did I leave behind?
Who remembers my name?
A tab left hanging,
The only reminder,
That I was ever here,
An empty stool tomorrow night,
Soon to be filled,
A replacement of sorts,
Can he pay my tab?
Or forever to be left hanging,
A reminder of me,
The equivalent of the park bench plaque,
For the alcoholic,
No blot to remind people of me,
Is it all I'm worth?
Just the price of my bill.

8th July 2005

My life so far

Here's my life so far,
Rock bottom was hit long before,
I struggle free from this pit,
Thrown in over again,
Rejection after rejection beat me back down,
Formed to this emotional cripple by those who should know better,
By those I was born to,
And by one promised to me by vows she made,
Constricted and contorted by the box I live in,
Turning into this grotesque emotional freak,
Is this just my failure to admit to my own faults?
Never facing the truth,
Running further from hurt,
Caused by my own inability to love,
Do you feel the icy cold to your touch?
Does my gaze send that chill through your spine?
Do you mistake it for attraction?
Can your touch thaw me before I freeze you?
Sending your emotions into stasis,
Seeing your feelings shut down,
But that's just me,

The icy Midas,
Not intended,
Just the side effects of being with me,
I start with all the best intentions,
But just like the snowman,
I chill your very soul,
Bring me to the sunlight and let it warm my skin,
Melt away this frozen grip from around my heart,
Bring my life back on track,
Just give me the time I need to step back into the light,
Away from this darkness that shrouds my life,
To return to humanity,
Not to live as this disturbing hermit,
Cellular and insular in this world of whispers and echoes,
Shadows move in the dark,
Ears straining to hear the whispers in this silence,
Eyes straining to glimpse the merest of light,
Living in this self-imposed cave,
Feeling my way through to find a way out,
This is the progress of my life,
This is my life so far.

9th July 2005

To my children

My mind drifts back,
To times spent together,
Warming hands in mine,
So small and fragile,
Forever wanting to protect,
But now in absence my heart breaks,
Memories remain strong,
I miss watching you grow,
I miss your tender glances,
Your love forever tattooed on my soul,
You turned this worthless man,
Into a father of joy,
Basking in the summer,
Filled with your devotion,
Our lives entwined,
Like the snakes,
Forever to worship you,
You are my life,
My love,
My babies.

12th July 2005

Farewell to my Jo-Jo

Her golden hair reflecting sunbeams,
Eyes sparkle like diamonds set in her platinum skin,
Is it any wonder after all these years?
It's her face I see when I close my eyes,
Lonely hours spent regretting words and actions,
Decisions seemed right when viewed through rose-tinted beer
glasses,
Now condemned to a life of regret,
If I had worked a little harder to retain her love,
Instead of inflicting pain,
The stake of lost love to her heart,
Killing as a wooden stake would kill my demons,
Leaving me imprisoned in a cell of my own making,
Now drifting back through my memories,
The smile that lit a room,
Hair softer than silk,
Skin smoother than marble,
Creating in me ecstasy enough to make a man cry,
And all at once the penny drops,
With a bang,
Loud enough to wake even the most dead at heart,
I once had it all,

But now no longer wanted, desired or wished for,
How dead was I not to understand?
As I sit and watch my life drift out the door,
Others mean nothing to me,
I barely remember their names,
Looking through them to see you,
But never to find in searching,
Nothing comes close,
You are and always will be the one that got away,
Stories I tell as mythical as the unicorn,
But will I ever return to this nirvana,
Will I be lucky enough to win the prize a second time?
Like a gambler who tries in vain to regain his lucky streak,
I lose a little more at each turn of the cards,
From this pinnacle the only way was down,
Plummeting at speed earthly bound,
Never stopping at terra firma,
Go straight to hell, do not pass go,
Do not collect £200,
Free-fall to fiery depths,
Punishment for all my sins,
Complaisance,
Lethargy,
Narcissism,
Of noncommittal,
Once blessed,
Now cursed,
Consigned to wander in purgatory,
The only reward for my failings,
Facing facts once shied away from,
Staring my fears in the eyes,
Smile wiped from my face,

Sobering to life a little too slowly,
Finally to realise my errors,
But all too late,
Nothing feeling like it should,
And never will again.

12th July 2005

Another place, another time

Were we good together?
Did we fulfill?
Did we fall short?
Does another we still continue unending,
Happy, loving, dancing and enjoying,
Life with all its hard curves,
Teaching us day by day,
Where we all go wrong,
Skeleton of lost love,
Laying on the side of the dusty heartbreak highway,
Life that once breathed through,
Now gone forever,
Left bleached by sun and time,
Time we never had,
Will ours go the same way?
What tragedy we became,
We could have been good,
But not to be,
Maybe in another place,
Perhaps in another time,
But just not this time or place,

Calamity only for us,
The years between us our undoing,
A love that should never have been,
If we were to be honest,
You still rule my night,
And pester my days,
You scorched my psyche,
And pulsed through my inner being,
Permanent as scars,
Addictive as nicotine,
I have used women to remove you from me,
Used drugs to let me sleep,
Drank, partied and played,
To only ill effect,
Inflicted with you as permanent as cancer,
In the nicest possible way,
Now left,
Like a shipwreck lying silently,
Image askew,
In the depths undisturbed,
Not looking for another shark,
Just another angel fish like you,
In another place,
In another time,
Would we have worked?

12th July 2005

Unsung heroes

What unsung heroes are these?
Behind the scenes we battle,
On all your high days and holidays,
Sweating and toiling in ever-rising heat,
Your pleasure is all we crave,
But tempers rise and flare,
The cooking clown in the corner relentless,
Jollying along the boys below,
We all do it for love and lust,
Smells and flavours abound,
Permeating through every corner of our miniature universe,
Through the vents and freed to the heavens,
Crashing and banging goes unheard,
The normal daily clatter of busy chefs,
Sauces bubble and reduce,
Flavour intensifying as the minutes pass,
Using all of our senses we work,
Taste, smell, feel and look,
All the pieces are ready,
We approach the plate as a virgin canvas,
Excitement rises as bit by bit we build,

Will it work?
Will it pass the boss's scrutiny?
The man at the front, he says yes,
We look and dissect,
Can we improve?
Of course we can, and do,
Striving for perfection every time,
But if it was easy,
Everyone would do it,
Those who can do, those who can't eat out,
Last check goes,
Heats turned off,
And we clean down,
One last fag break to recollect and pool our thoughts,
We all still buzz as the adrenalin ebbs away,
Feet ache and mental tension gives way to fatigue,
Hats and jackets saturated, we reminisce,
And as for tomorrow,
Well, we will do it all again.

14th July 2005

Tattoos

As I begin the journey,
Butterflies start to tickle,
After seven visits it's still there,
Nerves or excitement,
Still I'm no clearer,
The bell rings above the door,
Hit by the sterile smell,
Taking me back to a time,
Still I can't grasp when,
The background noises of music and buzzing,
I sit and wait for my time,
Scanning walls of artistic graffiti,
Random but with purpose,
Highly coloured but monochrome,
I rise, heading down steps,
To sit in front of him, gun in hand,
Inks stand by,
Transfer ready,
Arm shaved with expert intent,
Outline on, are you ready,
Buzzing starts and comes closer,
Stabbed by the needle, leaving its permanent mark,

So to put myself through this once more,
Was only going to have the one,
But it's so addictive,
And I was warned they would be,
Concentration at its utmost,
Don't slip now, no eraser can remove,
More guns start around the room,
Making the place buzz,
Human canvases we are,
Carrying their art with us,
Forever to show the world,
A world not yet ready to accept us and our choices,
But still we return again and again,
At last it's finished, washed and ointment applied,
We both look admiringly,
That okay, he asks,
Too late now if it's not, I think,
But as usual it's perfect,
And my mind begins to think of the next one,
How many more will I have?
I'm not sure,
How long till I'm finished,
Till I have perfected god's original creation,
Ring and needles will see me again,
As I leave I tell Gary I will see him next time,
I'm never going to be a Mona Lisa,
That's true,
It just makes my body easier to identify in the morgue,
Love them or hate them,
I don't care,
Just accept me for who I am,
Don't judge this book by its cover,
As expertly as it's drawn,

See my illustrations and notice,
And if you're willing to go past the cover,
You will find,
It's a magical pop-up book.

14th July 2005

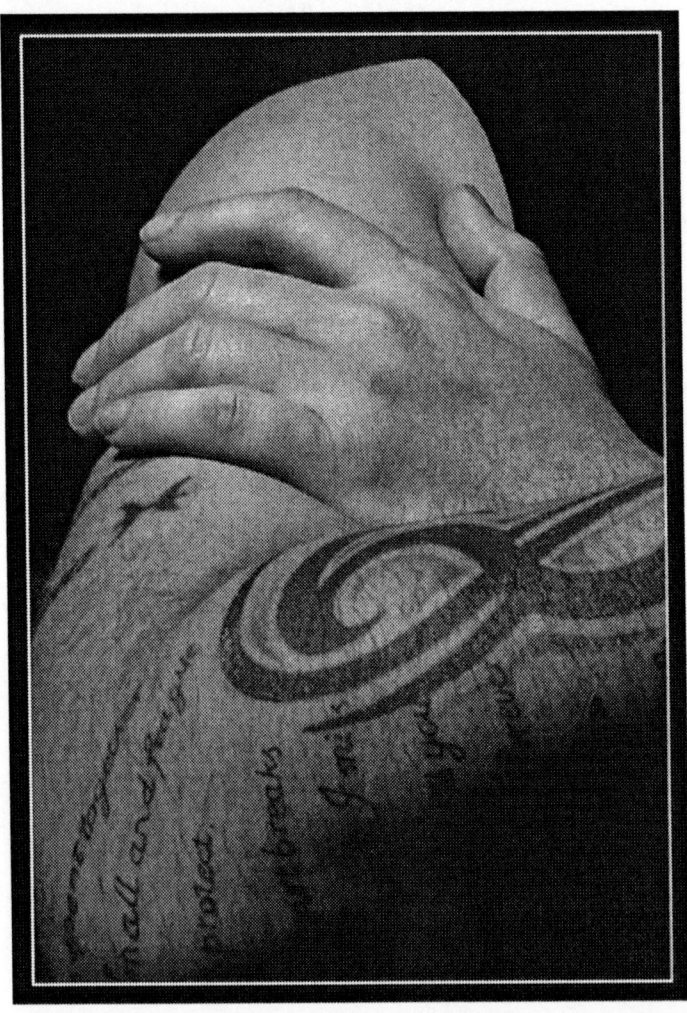

My reflection

I see my face,
Bounced back from the reflection in a pool,
So clear and sharp,
Not a breath blows to shimmer the surface,
But how did I change,
Is it as simple as a slight touch?
Or as heavy as a large stone,
To make the pool ripple,
And my appearance change,
Did a light finger's touch change it?
To this blurred and fractured image,
Or the lightest pond skater to reveal the inner me,
How did it change my outward image to others?
Did they already know?
Just waiting for the evidence,
Or do I still refute the claim I'm not what I appear,
That the water just distorts,
Or do I claim life in its unfairness,
Paints me wrong,
Does the mermaid still remember my image before the storm?
Or do I have to bluff,
Hoping not to be called on the hand of life,

Or just fold and walk away,
But how shallow are we talking,
A muddy puddle,
Or the vast ocean,
Whatever, I hope to reach bottom soon,
After that there is only one way,
But in the drowning,
Lungs burst and eyes bulge,
Heart speeds and skips,
I look up and see the sun,
Dancing through the surface and split into rainbows,
Faces of my past looking down,
Knowing in drowning,
In this pool of self-abhorrence,
Pulled down by my inner demons.
Closer each day to the gravelly bottom,
Sand to suck me deeper,
Hand of my past pulling me further in,
Till my light is totally engulfed,
Let me awake from this unscathed,
But that's not to be,
Like the picture of Dorian Gray,
It's my sleep that's haunted,
And my mortality unaffected,
Though my mind is destroyed night by night,
A little more each day the monsters surface,
Quicker and quicker,
Till rage rules my life,
Compassion gone totally,
But yet my reflection remains.

15th July 2005

No man's an island

Do we go through this life just brushing by?
In a frictionless dance,
Or do we ever connect,
Touching each other's spirituality,
Are we just merely floating islands?
Brushing,
Touching,
Never to linger long,
To communicate,
Blessed are we with humanity,
With communication,
Damned are we to build walls for protection,
That lead to isolation and despair,
We show masks to others we want them to see,
With no honesty and truth,
We never trust,
Just pretend to be,
Finding and trying to fill this earthly void,
Or are we just filling time and punching the clock,
In this living torment we create,
Or are we just another organism to procreate,

A mere tool to extend life,
With delusions of grandeur and civilization,
Just animals pretending to be what we are not,
Pretending we can control our fears,
Should we return to fields of green?
Roaming and grazing,
Free in freedom,
Not bricked up in castles of stone,
Working for paper and metal,
To build more walls.
We spend time in hurt and hurting,
Ones we love,
Ones we hate,
Crossing lanes of love and hate on a whim,
Or do we hate the ones we love,
Or love those we hate,
Do we therefore hate everyone?
Pessimist or realist,
Renegade or robot,
Following commands of what we call civilised,
Will we be pillared and crucified for thinking,
To believe is to be human, as is to be wrong,
To kill and fight is animal,
But we do it in righteousness,
For sovereign or god,
Do we sanction ourselves to the masses?
Are we afraid to be us?
A need to conform,
Or are we just intelligent sheep,
Afraid to cross the lions of prestige and power,
As we evolved we descend further to tribalism,
Are we devolving?

Returning to the animals we run from,
The well of human kindness bled dry,
Just dust and stone hearts remain,
Compassion and joy encased in glass,
Viewed for the entry fee,
Of memories past,
Feelings extinct,
Told about in dusty volumes,
In silence never to be removed.

16th July 2005

Running away

The moon watches over my night's journey,
Heather-clad hills roll on,
The sky as black as coal, sparkling with mineral flecks,
Trees whisper to each other, plotting my course
Ghosts of my past come raging and uncontrolled,
Out of the night air on swirling black clouds of hopelessness,
My life for all its years packs into a single car,
Trying to outrun these apparitions that trouble me,
Haunting my days one after another,
Leading me to this eventual despair,
In the mirror I see,
They gain on me mile by mile,
Finding me again,
Am I unable to outrun these spirits?
My speed increases,
Trees, fields and hills now just a blur,
And still they gain,
Faces covered in dark, musky shrouds,
Skeletal hands supporting long, sharp talons,
Once again to score and furrow my mortal flesh,
To tear and torture my frail mind,

Whispering to me of loss and pain,
Insane laughter as I writhe and twist,
Agonising through every moment of the day,
Never to be silenced or misplaced,
The blackened sky now with streaks of deep red,
Night gives way to dawn,
Slowly, not wanting to relinquish,
Its grip over the land slowly disappearing,
Deep scarlet giving way to deep oranges,
To warming golden tones,
Life wakes around me,
Birds sing me good morning,
And just for a moment lost,
The world in all its beauty embraces me,
Warm and tender as its touch,
Pain gone and troubles forgot,
And in this moment of oneness with life,
My guard dropped, leaving me vulnerable and defenceless,
They pounce to remind me,
Burning into me searing and uncontrollable,
My running over,
Now just to be overrun once again,
They whisper to me in a gurgling sigh,
Breath of something long dead hangs on the air,
You can run is the message,
You can hide,
But never from yourself.

20th July 2005

Life, the universe and everything

This small speck of dust,
Amongst millions of stars,
They sparkle and burst around us,
Planets revolve as do we,
Circling that huge ball of fire,
Like moths to the flame,
As we move in,
This planet called earth,
Men and animals running round in perpetual circles,
Like ants trapped behind glass,
In petulance we live,
Hating those who differ from us,
By the colour of your skin,
The man you pray to,
The team you support,
The school you go to,
The avenue you live on,
Is he up there looking down in dismay?
Is he laughing at the hell we put each other through,
Just in order to survive,
To get to the top of the heap,

What's it all about,
Will we ever find the answers we seek?
Will we ever live in harmony?
Or is it this dissonance we crave,
Like a drug it grabs you and pulls you into it,
Decaying you from inside out,
Till right from wrong is no longer clear,
Lines merge and mingle in surreal complexity,
Are we slowly dying out little by little?
Each generation we dwindle, killing us by fractions,
As each century passes,
Or will the powers that be find a new toy to torment,
And squish us like the bug and your newspaper,
Is there any hope for mankind?
Should we just quit and let another being have its chance,
As we evolve we become more animal,
Will animals evolve to be more human?
Or will we just destroy our planet first,
Just from sheer peevishness,
In our perpetual tantrum with life,
Men of power sitting with the fingers on buttons,
To blow us all to the ends of time,
Can they really be so sightless?
I hear the piano playing in the wings,
The play of life reaches its curtain call,
Do we have time for one last bow?
Arching down to view our feet,
Humble in the sight of others,
Why do we feel the need to make it so hard?
To love and lose,
To live and die,

In a world of such incomparable beauty,
Why do we not take time to enjoy?
Or has our hatred putrefied our very souls,
Would the next contender for this planet please stand up,
Your time is almost here.

21st July 2005

Autumn

The autumn trees changing colour,
Sun mellowing to deep gold,
Shards of light cascading through,
Resonating vibrant light and colours,
Summer wheat now gone,
Just stubble left to show,
Waiting its turn to be ploughed into the damp late-season earth,
Waning months pass,
Sun hangs lower in the evening sky,
Wave goodbye to summer,
Now into transformation,
Days in turn shorten minute by minute,
The first breath of winter chill on summer's fading gasp,
The once-soft spring leaves full of life and promise,
Now fall at my feet and rustle,
Dry and gone, their time now passed,
But beauty still remains,
Deep in thought, kicking through leaves,
The soft smell of November fires drifts on the breeze,

Winter moments away,
Bright lights and decorated trees nearly upon us,
But for now,
Just let us enjoy,
And remember,
Summer in its full glory,
The soundtrack to our own summers,
Ringing in our ears,
At night when we close our eyes,
We are there again,
Dancing, laughing,
And we know summer love don't last,
But still we cling,
Every teen movie ever seen,
It works there, why not here,
I awake and look,
Through the window,
Once magical and looking out to summer long,
Now just to see ageing trees balding,
A dull and lifeless world,
Holidays remembered only in photographs,
Wardrobe changed for the oncoming season,
No one stopping long enough to notice the beauty I see,
Living each season as it maybe my last,
Childlike in my apprehension,
Enjoying as each leaf hits my brow,
It has its own pungent smell,
But comforting to my soul,
If I catch another leaf will this wish come true?
No,
To live another season alone,

Christmas list shortens,
Do I love autumn?
Yes, I do.

22nd July 2005

In a galaxy far, far away

I hear an angel softly singing,
Just out of reach,
From afar,
Memories from my past,
Stirred and too unpleasant to be awakened,
Just ghosts from ancient times,
Loves of my past, soft and warm,
In good times and better,
From bad to worse to unbearable,
No spark to be found like the first,
And I believe there never will,
Will I forever stroll through life with flame extinguished,
Who can relight this torch?
One that once burned brighter than any sun,
Now put out by a gallon or more of black nectar,
A weakness I admit,
Social pariah I am not,
This monkey on my back tries to cripple,
I build more walls to save me,
If only from myself,
As time passes,

I lose more social skills,
I build castles of sand,
Each night to be washed away,
The ever-encroaching tide destroys all I build,
Bringing pain in its wake,
To shake me to foundations too shallow to support,
Each day a struggle to rebuild,
Like treading water in a sea of molasses,
Going nowhere but down,
Sickly sweet in its touch and taste,
I feel my life ebb away more each day,
Any humanity lost long before,
Take this shell of a man,
Refill my desire and lust for this world,
Shade my mind's eye from visions of the next life,
Replenish my soul with the kindness it once knew,
Blinker me from the atrocities of mankind,
Fill me with the hope of childhood,
Shield me from the ugliness of human nature,
And pain of this life,
Let me believe in hope,
Let me believe in life,
As infectious as it can be,
Can I inflict the world with it?
If not,
Let me live in a galaxy far, far away.

26th July 2005

To be honest

What strange phrase is this?
Used by many,
Meant by none,
But just for once,
As refreshing as lemonade on a hot August day,
I will be,
Honest,
Honestly,
In pure honesty,
Truthful, gov,
Straight up,
Stab me in the eye,
Should I tell lie,
I'm in love,
Have been for many years,
It was my first love,
My only love,
She has hair as golden as the most beautiful sunrise,
Eyes bluer than the deepest ocean,
A smile that could light a galaxy for a millennia,
A heart as immense as any ocean,

And we were happy,
For a short while in the spectrum of life,
But,
I lost her,
No one to blame but me,
Now lost and alone,
A solitary star in the night sky,
Cold and lifeless,
Shining for all to see,
Masking well what I feel and do,
Actions furthering me from my love,
Never closer
Unable to reveal to those closest,
Never wanting to lose,
This image of nonchalance,
Which I wear so well to face the world outside,
It's Alan,
He's a good old boy,
They think,
Envious of this seemingly carefree life I live,
But between me,
And the fly on the wall,
We know the truth,
And this is where it will remain,
To take to my beckoning grave,
This secret I will take,
And a million years of silence will keep it,
I love you,
Have and always will be in love with you,
Time and tide wait for no man,
Least of all me,
And as we drift further from each other,

Just believe,
I love you.
And always will,
But can't show you my heart,
Just because,
Honestly,
I love you and always will,
Honest.

27th July 2005

The answer to your dreams?

View me as you will,
But all I ask,
Don't judge this book by my cover,
Between these pages you may find,
All your hopes and prayers answered,
For under this exterior,
With all its marks and scars,
Is where the real me exists,
Like a animal in a cave,
Hidden and shy,
To be encouraged out,
In time you may see the real person,
Lingering in the dark, away from hate and ridicule,
The mocking of others wounding and belittling,
Making me reticent about human contact,
Making this solitary life all I want,
My inner self looking for the warm touch,
Softly spoken words and tender fingertips,
Is all my heart's desire,
My mind a little more wary,
Remembering a past of pain and put-downs,

Left to linger in the bottom of a glass,
And where I will stay if only for the ease,
For it's there my life will end,
My light turned off from self-will,
Begging for the reaper's touch,
Long before my time,
Leaving me to suffer,
To tear myself apart from inside out,
Ripping and tearing at my mind for answers,
Dreaming night after night,
The faceless woman who will save me,
Bringing me back to the light,
Showing the trail of crumbs of my past persona,
Shattered and rejected,
Lying on the dusty floor, kicked and ignored,
Passers-by to wonder,
Who this once was so confident and assured,
Now broken and disregarded,
So here I am,
You get more than you see,
Look upon me with innocent eyes,
See me for who I am,
And not who you think I should be,
I could be,
If given time,
The answer to your dreams.

27th July 2005

My redemption song

This is my life's journey through my eyes,
The only perspective I know,
Here are my hopes through my dreams,
Here are my fears through my experiences,
Just to find my redemption through my words,
Are you fit to judge my actions?
Are you better than me?
So uncontaminated to give opinions,
Is this life I lead so very wrong?
Is the life I have led so appalling?
Is my redemption just moments away,
Or will I have to wait,
Till angels sing my way to the final deliverance,
My only road to emancipation from my sins,
Done unto others to punish myself,
Is it my will to remain alone?
Do I need to bleed this way?
Some bizarre punishment administered by self-will,
By a need of emotional self-cleansing,
Tears of isolation roll from these bloodshot eyes,
Callously burning my face in their wake,

Salty to taste,
Crusting trails left to show their journey,
My blackened heart lifeless and drained of blood,
Bled by the vampire of solitude,
To live unconscious in a vacuous void,
Nothingness fills my waking moments,
A vast blackness fills my nights,
I float through unaware,
Straining eyes that never adjust,
The only sound is strained breathing,
But I find peace,
Tranquillity in this seclusion,
Welcoming and pleasant,
But don't judge me on who I am,
Think of me as I could be,
They all pass me by,
Not seeing,
They look straight through me,
Am I just a figment of my own hyperactive imagination?
An apparition of smoke and dust,
Reflection of light-giving substance,
But now to free my mind to the heavens once more,
I ignite and smoke this special blend,
Clouds of coloured haze fill my consciousness,
And here within my surrealism,
I find my redemption.

28th July 2005

Greymen

Everywhere I look,
There they are,
Standing on street corners,
Waiting to cross the roads,
Standing there in grey plaid,
Grey ties,
Their grey complexions blending in,
There is no colour in their world,
Forcing their grey values onto the world at large,
Bringing grey to our lives,
Seeping in every crack,
Through the TV,
Through the airwaves,
Exterminating colour from our world,
Pockets of bright kaleidoscopic beams hide in secret,
Huddling round the spectrum,
Keeping the colours alive,
Nurturing its growth,
Till one day we burst back,
Bringing rainbows back to life,
Cascading colours rolling down the waterfall,

Sunrise and set brought back to full glory,
But for now,
Shy away,
Do not contaminate with grey,
Forever carry your colour in your pocket,
Keep it in your heart,
Bring it forth when the grey age is at an end,
Release and let that butterfly flutter away,
Spreading effervescence across the sky,
Bringing smiles to the face of those view them,
Banishing grey from this universe,
So till then,
Carry your colour between your eyes.

29th July 2005

My problem

I feel my persona changing,
Unlike drugs in so many ways,
Couple of swift ones,
Changing me in a way I'm not sure of,
In so many ways I'm not happy with,
Ears buzz with alcohol,
Night air scented with wisps of acidic tones,
As the darkness gasps against my flushed skin,
Hot to touch I feel,
Pavement swims and twists,
My internal cockney ever more present,
Descending into a life from long ago,
To live within forever on and off,
This disease I have,
No cure except from inside,
But there it lurks, hiding away from prying eyes,
Covered with this mask of normality,
No external blemishes to give me away,
But riddled with it I still am,
Like a cancer it spreads through me,
Just one whiff from the doorway to my heaven,

Music from inside floats out,
Voices and laughter make it more acceptable,
Lying to myself begins from here,
And will continue deep in to the nocturnal hours,
Till my legs no longer stabilize me,
This creeping paralysis takes me over,
Muscles give up and beg for no more,
My brain is the only semi-functioning organ,
Willing my body to continue, never letting go,
Oblivious to the torture I am in,
Rehearsing the phrases I will need,
Changing and infecting my mind,
Turning me into what I am not,
Or try not to be,
I never wanted to be this person,
But this is who I have become,
Creeping up on me with stealth,
Unknowing of its approach,
Until it's too late to run,
Like the antelope in the lion's gaze,
Torn and ripped apart,
Disembowelled and disembodied,
Bloodied and bruised by the invading looter,
Left for dead,
But only in spirit,
For come sunrise,
My punishment will become clear.

30th July 2005

In absence

Marked with an x,
In the register of life,
Totally absent from the human race as it stands,
With no great regret I fear,
Not that it's a shame,
A loner in the scheme of things,
With no remorse of things done unto others,
Although the shame pangs,
In the back of my mind,
The feeling is papered over and obscured,
Forgotten and moved on,
Am I human?
Or just an observer to this race,
My atrocities pale into insignificance,
When we are viewed from the expanse of space,
Or from this battered armchair,
As one of the MTV generation,
Twenty-four-hour global news,
With no certificate for innocent eyes,
The menu of life laid out in well-spoken accents,
I wish to be absent from this,

Bombs and death,
War and famine,
Wall-to-wall bloodshed,
For all to see,
Will we survive or perish,
What example do we set to our future?
Do we even have one?
Do we deserve one?
Are we watched by other life forms?
I certainly hope not.

31st July 2005

Reality?

What is this pap we watch?
Reality?
Only in the most commercial sense,
Is it escapism?
Or just a compulsive vacuum,
Devoid of worth or legitimate intent,
Camera rolls twenty-four/seven,
To watch people in isolation,
Masks they wear never to be seen through,
Acting and pretending through waking hours,
But still like sheep we follow,
Kidding ourselves that it's unplanned,
Voyeurism in its most unadorned form,
This borderline perversion,
Each year passes we change,
Becoming a nation of legitimate peeping toms,
Raving at the glimpse of bare flesh,
Cheering at tempers flared,
Like caged animals we encourage their taunting,
Forgetting all the values that make our society civilized,
Thirteen weeks of savage instinct,

Bubble up through our souls,
Just a flick of the button and we are there,
Glued to the screen waiting,
But for what?
Does it fulfil a need in our lives?
Something missing within our own four walls,
This bland and tasteless offering,
Reality's answer to Soylent Green,
Yet we still live our lives through others.

1st August 2005

Sax appeal

There he sits,
Glistening in sunbeams,
Casting reflections of light across the room,
Projecting flashes on the wall,
Bathing the corner in golden light,
And there he stays,
Inanimate and lifeless,
Waiting,
Ever ready for the attention,
A chance to fulfil his potential,
His heavy, dead weight a sign of craftsmanship,
But when brought to life,
With lungs of air,
Its deep and melancholy song will rise,
To the heavens it floats,
From the glistening brass bell,
Making angels envious at its god-like sigh,
Breathing air into a resonating exhale,
Reverberation making us one with the song,
Through our limbs into our mind,
Filtering to our very soul,

Lifting our hearts,
Rising with the melody into the atmosphere,
The mantra ends,
Back to earth we plummet,
Returned to his corner till next time,
Now that's sax appeal.

1st August 2005

Do trees scream?

Do trees scream?
Living and growing,
Feeling and fearing,
Provided for the planet,
To the planet,
Bringing beauty and wonder to our world,
Getting stronger as we decay,
Watching us grow and devour,
More life by lifetime,
As the rainforests disappear,
One by one,
Our desire for their meat ever growing,
Another table, another chair,
Destroying them tree by tree,
They raise their screech to the heavens,
Birds and bugs retreat,
Their refuge ever shrinking,
They the only ones to understand what's yelled,
But will they yield,
To us, no,
Can you hear it?

Ssshhh,
Listen,
It's whispered on the wind,
It's rustled through the branches,
They see our demise in their wisdom,
Do they scream?
Would we still do it?
If we could hear them.

5th August 2005

Printed in the United Kingdom
by Lightning Source UK Ltd.
119853UK00001B/75